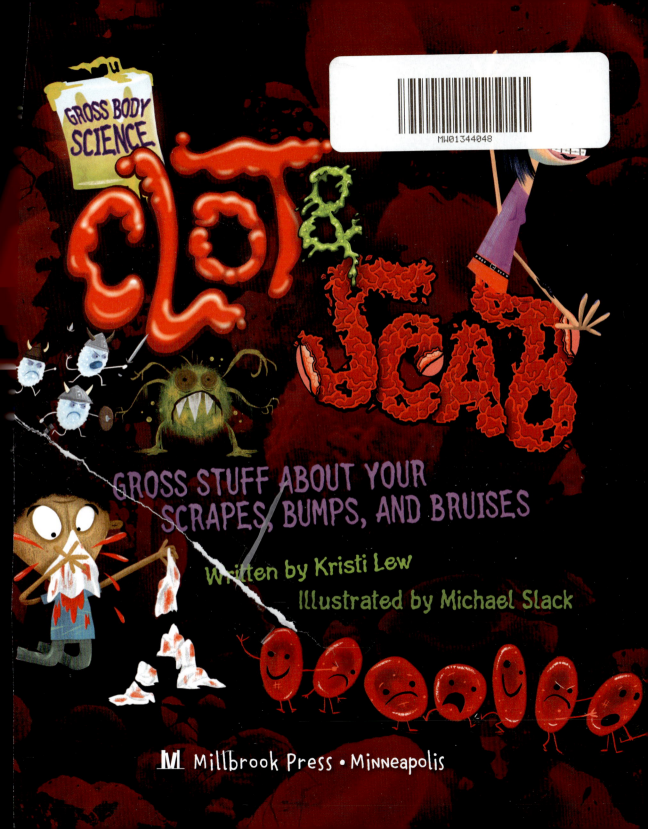

To Simon, thanks for your
unique perspective
-Kristi Lew

To Phylleen and Brooke
-Michael Slack

Text copyright © 2010 by Kristi Lew
Illustrations copyright © 2010 by Michael Slack

All rights reserved. International copyright secured. No part of this book may be reproduced, stored in a retrieval system, or transmitted in any form or by any means—electronic, mechanical, photocopying, recording, or otherwise—without the prior written permission of Lerner Publishing Group, Inc., except for the inclusion of brief quotations in an acknowledged review.

Millbrook Press
A division of Lerner Publishing Group, Inc.
241 First Avenue North
Minneapolis, MN 55401 USA

For reading levels and more information, look up this title at www.lernerbooks.com.

Library of Congress Cataloging-in-Publication Data

Lew, Kristi.
   Clot & scab : gross stuff about your scrapes, bumps, and bruises / by Kristi Lew ; illustrations by Michael Slack.
     p. cm. — (Gross body science)
   Includes bibliographical references and index.
   ISBN 978–0–8225–8965–5 (lib. bdg. : alk. paper)
   ISBN 978–0–7613–8108–2 (eb pdf)
   1. Wound healing—Juvenile literature. 2. Wounds and injuries—Juvenile literature. 3. Bruises—Juvenile literature. I. Slack, Michael H., 1969– ill. II. Title. III. Title: Clot and scab.
RD94.L49 2010
617.1—dc22   2008045626

Manufactured in the United States of America
6-51200-9118-6/16/2021

CONTENTS

CHAPTER 1
SCRAPES, SCABS, AND SCARS
Shredding Your Skin   page 4

CHAPTER 2
STICKY, RED, AND FULL OF LIFE
Blood's Everybody's Buddy   page 13

CHAPTER 3
FLOW, GUSH, AND POOL
All about Bleeding   page 23

CHAPTER 4
STOP, CLOT, AND ROT
The Flow Stops Here   page 34

Glossary **42**
Selected Bibliography **43**
Further Reading **44**
Index **47**

CHAPTER 1
SCRAPES, SCABS, and SCARS

SHREDDING YOUR SKIN

Have you ever fallen off your bike and dragged some poor body part along the pavement? **YOW!** Not only does it hurt like crazy, it looks nasty too. But don't worry. While you made hamburger out of your knee or elbow, your body got busy repairing the damage.

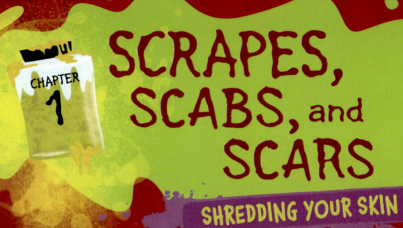

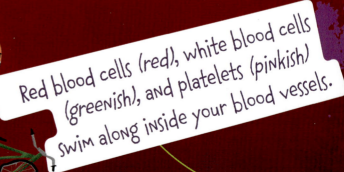

Red blood cells (red), white blood cells (greenish), and platelets (pinkish) swim along inside your blood vessels.

GROSS FACT #1

Platelets and other blood cells are made in the squishy tissue that fills the inside of bones. This tissue is called bone marrow. Some people eat bone marrow. They might crack open animal bones and suck the marrow right out of the bone. Other times, the marrow is cooked first. People say that cooked marrow tastes salty and fatty, sort of like butter. But unlike butter, the marrow has a slimy texture like boogers. **YUMMY,** pass those bones!

THANKS A CLOT!

As soon as you rip a hole in your skin, your blood gets to work. It starts by rushing special cells, called platelets, to the point of injury. Platelets are like your body's glue. They gather at the place of the wound and make a sticky glob called a **CLOT**. A clot is like a plug to stop the bleeding. If your blood does not clot, you could bleed to death. Even from something minor, like a scraped knee or an elbow—talk about a bad day!

Platelets don't do it alone. As they're plugging the injury, they're also sending a shout-out to other chemicals in the body. **"YO! A LITTLE HELP OVER HERE!"** The other chemicals they're calling are clotting proteins. When those clotting proteins get the signal, they come running to the wounded area.

After the clotting proteins arrive, they get right to work. They help the platelets make a web. This web helps to hold the platelet plug in place. Blood cells

GROSS FACT #2
Platelets age fast! If a platelet is not used to stop up a cut within ten days after the platelet is made, it dies.

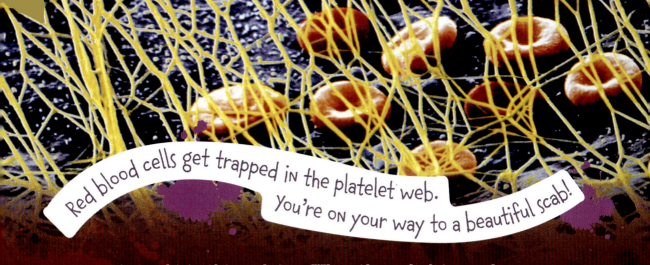

Red blood cells get trapped in the platelet web. You're on your way to a beautiful scab!

get caught in this web too. When the web dries and hardens, it forms a scab. The blood cells caught in the web give the scab its lovely reddish brown color. Yep, scabs are just a big **BLOODY PLUG**. But before you get too grossed out, think of it this way: scabs are also your body's bandages. They protect the new skin that's forming under them.

HELP YOUR BODY HEAL

To help your body heal the way it is meant to, you have to eat a healthy diet. To plug up wounds and make new skin, the body needs calcium, vitamin K, and vitamin C. Keeping wounds covered and moist will help them heal faster too. So stop picking at that scab!

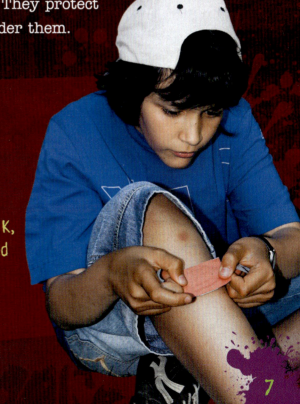

BLOODY SAYINGS

SAYING	WHAT DOES IT MEAN?
That makes my blood boil!	That makes me mad!
Bloodthirsty	Eager to see violence
Hot-blooded	Someone who gets mad easily
Cold-blooded	Someone who is very cruel or mean
Bloodbath	A battle with many deaths
Blue blood	Having a wealthy or royal background

SCARS

Ah, what could be lovelier than a **BIG BLOODY SCAB**? Thankfully, scabs are only temporary. They stick around just long enough to help the healing. By the time your body has stopped the gushing flow of blood, the healing process is well under way. Once a scab forms, your body is already making new skin. Sometimes when the scab falls off, the new skin looks different from the other skin around it. That's because it's a scar.

Here's a nice, crusty scab. It's the first step in your skin's healing process.

Check out this keloid scar!

Most scars are flat and pale. In other words, **BOR-ING!** But sometimes scars get quite interesting looking. Some are raised or bumpy. Those are called keloid. Other scars look like pits or craters in the skin. These sunken scars are most often caused by acne, chicken pox, or—ow!—surgical cuts. Depending on your point of view, these are either really cool or really gross!

Puffy, dented, smooth, or jagged...whatever kind of scars you end up with, you'll get to enjoy those beauties for a long time. Even if they fade over time, they'll probably never totally go away. Actually, it can be pretty fun to compare road rash with your buddies. You'll always have a good story to tell about each one.

When a large cut heals, it can leave a flat or pitted scar.

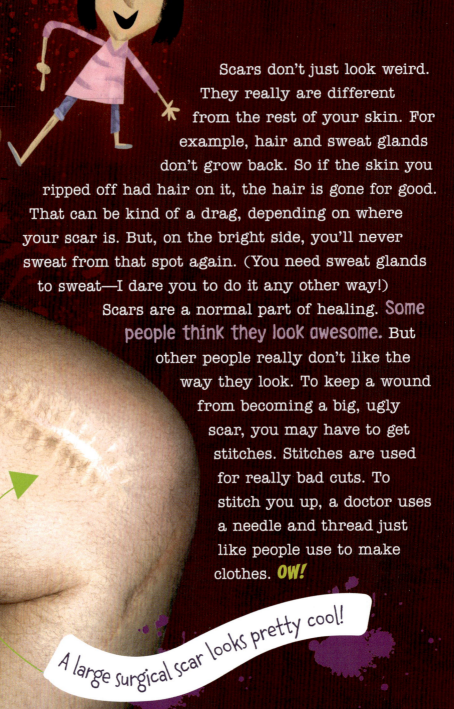

Scars don't just look weird. They really are different from the rest of your skin. For example, hair and sweat glands don't grow back. So if the skin you ripped off had hair on it, the hair is gone for good. That can be kind of a drag, depending on where your scar is. But, on the bright side, you'll never sweat from that spot again. (You need sweat glands to sweat—I dare you to do it any other way!)

Scars are a normal part of healing. Some people think they look awesome. But other people really don't like the way they look. To keep a wound from becoming a big, ugly scar, you may have to get stitches. Stitches are used for really bad cuts. To stitch you up, a doctor uses a needle and thread just like people use to make clothes. OW!

A large surgical scar looks pretty cool!

Here's what a stitch, or suture, looks like up close.

Luckily, doctors are expert sewers. They use two types of stitches to sew people up. One type must be taken out by your doctor a few days after they are put in. The other type is absorbed by your body after their job is done. That's right, one day you've got thread holding your body together and the next time you look—**YOWZA**, no stitches!

GROSS FACT #3

Some stitches are made out of a material called catgut. No, catgut is not really made from the family cat. But it is made from an animal's insides. Catgut is usually made out of specially treated cow or sheep intestine. The material is strong and easily absorbed by your body. Amazing! (And kind of gross.)

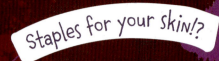

Staples for your skin!?

Instead of stitches, a doctor might just staple you up. Surgical staples look a lot like regular staples (only bigger). Stapling a wound shut is much faster than stitching one up with needle and thread. Now hold still... **KA-CHUNK!**

Stitches and staples help a wound heal faster. They also help make scars smaller. But the only way to absolutely avoid scars is to never hurt yourself. Good luck with that one!

GROSS FACT #4

Stapling wounds closed sounds gross, but it's nothing new. In ancient India, doctors didn't have metal staples as we do in modern times. So they had their own way of making staples. They put live ants or beetles on the edges of a wound. The animals pinched the wound shut with their mouths. Then the doctors cut the animals' bodies off. They left their mouths, or "staples," behind!

CHAPTER 2
STICKY, RED, and FULL OF LIFE

BLOOD'S EVERYBODY'S BUDDY

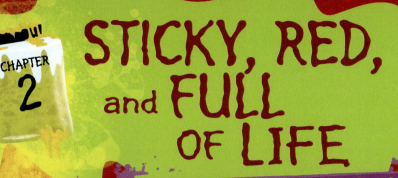

Skateboarding, bike riding, and soccer playing can sometimes be a bloody business. After all, you're not really having fun until you leave a chunk of yourself on the street or mix your blood with the mud, right? But where does all that red stuff come from?

A little bit of blood is nothing to cry about! But you should be sure to clean that wound and cover it with a bandage.

Blood gets pumped out of the heart through the red arteries to the rest of the body. It returns to the lungs through the blue veins.

PUMP IT UP

Blood is sometimes called the fluid of life. (And you thought soda pop was the fluid of life!) Blood carries nutrients and oxygen to the body's cells. Your body needs these things so it can grow. Sounds great, right? But blood also carries carbon dioxide. **CARBON DYE WHO?** Carbon dioxide. It's a chemical that your cells don't need. So how do they get rid of it? **They ship it off in the blood to the lungs.** And then, adios, amigo! Your lungs get rid of the unwanted stuff by breathing it out. Without blood, your body would stop working and you would die.

GROSS FACT #5
Picture five 1-liter bottles of soda pop lined up in a row. That's how much blood the average adult has running through his or her veins.

Blood moves throughout the body in hollow tubes called blood vessels. The heart, which is a powerful muscle in the chest, makes it go. When the heart squeezes, it pumps blood through the blood vessels all through the body. The heart and blood vessels make up the body's circulatory system.

You have three types of blood vessels. They are arteries, veins, and capillaries. Arteries carry the blood away from the heart and deliver it to other parts of the body. Veins carry the blood back to the heart. Together, arteries and veins are like highways for blood. **BUCKLE UP!**

The human heart is an amazing muscle!

GROSS FACT #6

If you ripped all the blood vessels out of your friend and put them end to end, they would stretch around Earth more than twice. **WARNING: THIS IS A GOOD WAY TO LOSE FRIENDS!**

Capillaries are very small, thin blood vessels that connect arteries and veins. **In fact, capillaries are so thin that blood cells can only go through them single file.** Kind of like lining up at school, only with no poking, shoving, or cooties. While blood moves through the capillaries, oxygen seeps out of them and into the body's cells where it is needed. In return, the cells send their carbon dioxide waste into the capillaries. What a trade!

HEY! No Pushing!

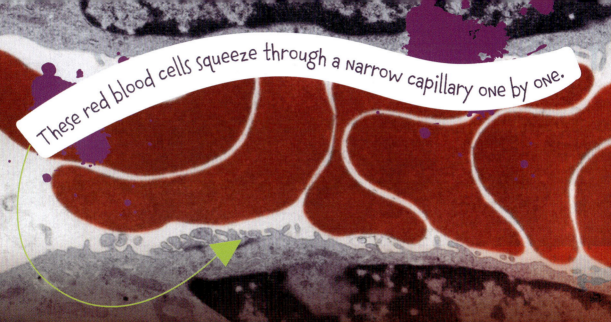

These red blood cells squeeze through a narrow capillary one by one.

After all that trading, the capillaries send the blood into the veins. The heart pumps it to the lungs. Then you breathe out the carbon dioxide and breathe in more oxygen. The oxygen goes into your blood, and the cycle starts all over again. A never-ending blood supply. This is the kind of stuff that vampires dream about.

Your body circulates blood day and night and never gets lazy or takes a break. And you thought cleaning your room seemed like a never-ending chore. Well, don't tell your parents how hard your body is working—they might get ideas about more chores.

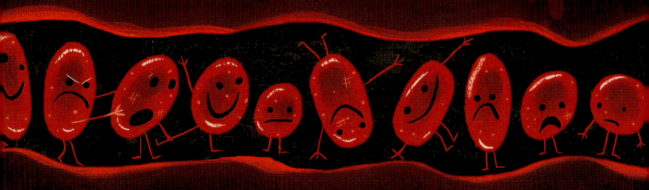

William Harvey figured out how blood circulates through the body.

CIRCULATORY HISTORY

Circulation was discovered by an English doctor named William Harvey. Harvey was fascinated with blood and the way it circulates. In 1628 he wrote a book describing how the heart pumps blood through the body.

At that time, people thought that the liver turned food into blood. And they thought the body ate its own blood for fuel! So people did not believe Harvey's ideas about blood circulation at first. They thought he was as nutty as a peanut butter sandwich. In fact, many of his patients stopped coming to see him.

Eventually, people realized Harvey was correct. Take that, nonbelievers! **WHO'S NUTTY NOW?**

GROSS FACT #7

It only takes a minute or two for your blood to make it all around your body and back to your heart.

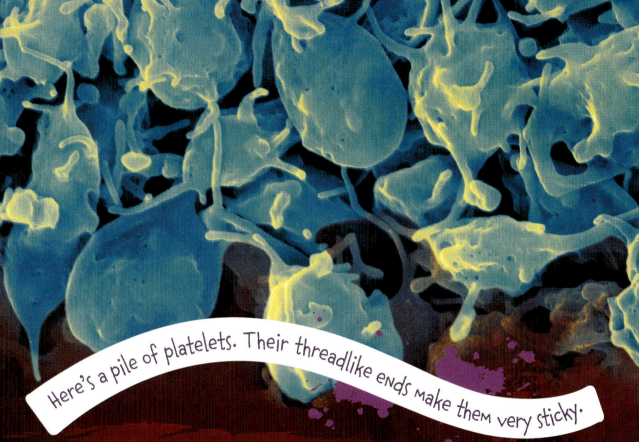

Here's a pile of platelets. Their threadlike ends make them very sticky.

WHAT'S IN BLOOD?

All mammals have red blood. When a mammal's blood is exposed to oxygen, it turns bright red. The color comes from a chemical in the blood called hemoglobin.

Blood contains three types of cells—platelets, red blood cells, and white blood cells. You remember platelets, right? Those blood cells that help you not bleed to death? Important little buggers. Red blood cells are important too. They contain the protein hemoglobin. Hemoglobin carries oxygen to the body's cells and takes carbon dioxide away from them.

BLOODWORMS

Ever seen one of these? They're bloodworms. Gross little things, aren't they? In spite of their name, bloodworms are not really worms. They are the larvae of the midge fly. They got their name because they look like bright red worms. That's because they contain a substance that is similar to hemoglobin.

Red blood cells are the most plentiful blood cells in our bodies. A normal adult has between 4 and 6 million red blood cells in 0.2 teaspoons (1 milliliter) of blood. Red blood cells live for about 120 days before dying and being replaced with other red blood cells.

White blood cells are the third type of blood cell. They help the body fight infection.

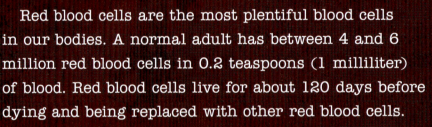

BLOOD OF OTHER COLORS

Not all animals have red blood. Horseshoe crabs have blue blood. That's because they don't have hemoglobin. A different protein carries oxygen in their bodies. Cockroaches do not carry oxygen in their blood at all. So their blood is colorless. Some marine worms have green blood. Awesome!

Staphylococcus aureus bacteria can cause a serious infection.

INFECTION

Scabs protect your body by keeping wounds clean. But sometimes germs get into your wound anyway. You're probably a pretty messy kid, letting all that dirt and germy stuff into your **BOO-BOOS**. Hey, it happens. Well, when it does, those germs can cause an infection. An infection can make you sick. Luckily, your body comes equipped with an immune system. Its job is to fight infections.

Your immune system knows when bacteria, viruses, or other microscopic meanies get inside your body. **As soon as it senses an invasion, the immune system calls on the body's soldiers—the white blood cells.** The white blood cells' job is to kill invaders like bacteria.

Here's a microscopic view of pus. It is made up of dead white blood cells.

If a cut gets infected, it sometimes swells up and oozes stuff called pus. Pus looks like sticky, clumpy gunk. **OOZING PUS MIGHT SEEM GROSS**, but it's a good sign. It means your immune system is working. And remember: Pus is not made up of the mayo you smeared on your bologna sandwich for lunch, so try not to eat it. It is made up of white blood cells that died in their battle against whatever invaded your body.

Pus, eew!

CHAPTER 3
FLOW, GUSH and POOL
ALL ABOUT BLEEDING

Usually your blood does a super job of clotting. But sometimes things go wrong. For example, if you get a really bad cut, even a healthy body can have problems stopping the bleeding. So be careful when playing with swords and battle-axes. They can give a nasty cut.

SEVERE BLOOD LOSS

Blood loss from a deep cut or other injury can quickly become dangerous if the bleeding can't be stopped. Applying pressure directly to the site of a cut will usually stop the bleeding. If the bleeding can't be stopped in fifteen minutes, you need to see a doctor. Then you have to explain to the doctor what you were doing with those swords and battle-axes.

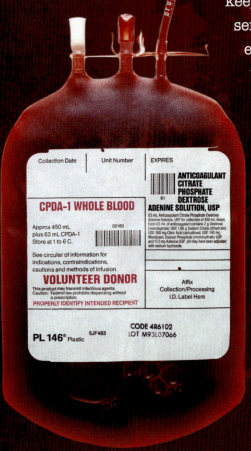

This bag of donated blood can be flowed into someone else who needs it.

That is, if you can stay awake. People who lose too much blood may feel dizzy and faint. If the bleeding keeps up, the person could be in serious trouble. Major problems or even death could result. To prevent that, a doctor may need to replace the blood the person lost. Doctors do this by giving the person a blood transfusion.

A transfusion means putting blood back into the body. The blood for a transfusion comes from another person. That person may be a relative or a stranger who gives blood to other people. Because the body constantly makes new blood cells, it is safe for adults to give away some of their 5 quarts (5 liters) of blood. Donated blood is stored in a blood bank until it is needed.

GROSS FACT #8
Every ten seconds, someone in the United States gets a blood transfusion.

BLOOD TYPES
Ever worry about how boring your meals would be if you were a vampire? Drinking the same old blood, night after night? Actually, a vampire's diet wouldn't be quite as boring as you might think. Not all human blood is the same. In fact, four different types exist. There's A, B, AB, and O. Each one has slightly different ingredients—proteins and other stuff on the surface of red blood cells. *MMM, SOUNDS YUMMY.*

25

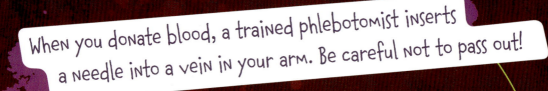

When you donate blood, a trained phlebotomist inserts a needle into a vein in your arm. Be careful not to pass out!

Blood types are genetic. That means that a person's blood type depends on what type blood their parents have. People who need a blood transfusion must receive the right type of blood. If they get the wrong type, their body will reject it and they can die. As for vampires, they could live off any blood type.

Now, ready to get confused? People who have type AB blood can receive any type blood. They are called universal recipients. But they can only give blood to people who have AB blood. People with type O blood, however, can give blood to anyone. They can run around town passing out their blood. "Here, have some blood." For this reason, people with type O blood are called universal donors. Only about 3 percent of Americans have AB blood. Almost half have type O.

NOSEBLEEDS

Everyone loves a good nosebleed now and then. **THE GORE, THE MESS**, the cleaning up. Fun stuff, right? Actually, most nosebleeds are harmless—though they can look really scary. It looks as if the poor person is losing gallons and gallons of blood. That's because the nose contains many blood vessels. And these vessels are very close to the surface. They are there to warm and moisten the air that you breathe in. But they can also spew out a lot of blood if you injure your nose.

The most common cause of nosebleeds is nose picking. Especially if you dig for **BOOGERS** in dry, winter weather. Of course, dry, winter weather makes the best dry, crusty nose oysters! But before you go digging for the tasty morsels, remember those easily damaged blood vessels. At the very least, please clip your fingernails. That'll keep you from ripping too many blood vessels.

BLOOD SQUIRTERS

Horned lizards have a strange way of defending themselves. To keep dogs, foxes, and coyotes from making the lizard their next meal, the horned lizard squirts blood from its eyes! The animals do not like the taste of the blood. They drop the lizard, and it scampers away. As you might imagine, the lizards try all sorts of things to get away from the dogs before they resort to blood squirting. But sometimes a lizard has to do what a lizard has to do!

HEMOPHILIA

Some people are born with a condition that keeps their blood from clotting at all. Their bodies do not make clotting proteins. This condition is called hemophilia. If a person with hemophilia gets a nosebleed or a scrape, it takes longer then usual for the bleeding to stop.

Extreme close-up of dried blood on a Band-Aid

MORE BLOODY WORDS

The study of blood is called hematology. Many other words that start with *hema-* or *hemo-* are blood related too. Hemorrhage, for example, means to bleed out of control. Hemostasis means to stop bleeding. A hematoma is a bruise. And a hemophobic is someone who is horribly afraid of blood.

Hemophilia is passed down in families. Every year about four hundred babies are born with hemophilia in the United States. Most of these babies are male. People who have hemophilia must give themselves shots that contain clotting proteins. The injected proteins will make their blood clot if they get hurt.

BLOODLETTING

Doctors in ancient times used to make people bleed on purpose. They believed bleeding could cure anything from a fever to mental illness. Got the sniffles? You might need a good bleeding. Headache? Bleed it out. Stubbed your toe? Let me find my knife. Kids back then probably didn't pretend to be sick to stay home from school. **THEY DIDN'T WANT TO GET SLICED OPEN!**

One way doctors got the blood flowing was with leeches. Leeches are bloodsucking worms. Doctors used them to reach places that their knives couldn't reach. Places like the gums, lips, or inside the nose, for example. **When was the last time you stuck a bloodsucking worm up your nose on purpose?** Or for that matter, by accident?

At least the patient could not feel the leeches latching onto their blood vessels. That's because leech spit has chemicals in it that numb the spot where they sink their little teeth. Those aren't the only chemicals in leech spit either. It also contains a chemical to keep the person's blood from clotting. This allows leeches to slurp from the **"ALL-YOU-CAN-DRINK" BLOOD BUFFET** as long as they like. They can get so full of blood that they grow up to ten times their normal size. After they finish, bloated leeches fall off the victim... whoops, I mean patient.

A leech latches on!

BLOODSUCKERS

Leeches are not the only bloodsucking critters out there. Vampire bats, mosquitoes, fleas, and ticks will all chow down on blood if given the chance. Like leeches, most of these animals have chemicals in their spit that keep the victim from feeling their bite until it is way too late. Also like leeches, they have anti-blood clotting chemicals in their spit.

Mosquitoes, fleas, and ticks actually suck blood. So do vampires—mwa ha haaaa! (Or they would, if they existed.) But vampire bats—which are not imaginary—do not suck blood. Instead, they lick it up. First, they use their razor-sharp teeth to cut open their victims. Then they lap up the pooling blood with their tiny little tongues. Aw, so cute! They hardly ever do this to humans, though. They prefer to feast on cows, horses, and pigs. That way there's a lot less screaming and swatting going on.

BRUISES

Not all bleeding occurs on the outside of the body. Remember the last time your so-called friend kicked you in the shin? Or the time you got smacked in the eye with a frozen fish? Or dropped a duck statue on your finger? You have to be careful with those duck statues.

Even if you're not this accident prone, you've probably had a big old bruise before. When your ex-best friend smacks you with a tennis racket, the impact can tear or break capillaries. Remember them? Capillaries are the tiniest blood vessels you have. When they get damaged, look out! Blood can leak out of them. The blood pools under the skin and shows through. That's the bruise you see. If this happens around your eye, you sport a big shiner for a couple of weeks!

Ow! That's quite a shiner!

Red blood cells ooze out of a torn capillary.

Bruises change color over time as the blood under the skin breaks down. They start out a reddish color. A couple days later, they turn purplish black. Pretty soon they take on a yellow green color, like **PUKE**. By the time two weeks have passed, bruises are usually light brown. After a bruise goes through the beautiful colors of the bruise rainbow, it finally disappears. All the blood has been reabsorbed by the body. **WHEW!**

As bruises age, they change color.

CHAPTER 4: STOP, CLOT, and ROT

THE FLOW STOPS HERE

While some health problems are caused by blood that will not stop flowing, others occur when blood does not flow the way it should. Blood clots are good if they stop you from losing too much blood. But some blood clots can cause major problems.

This clot has blocked a blood vessel. Blood clots can cause serious health problems.

BLOOD CLOTS INSIDE YOUR BLOOD VESSELS

Scabs are blood clots on the outside of our bodies. We can see them—and lucky for us, since they are so beautiful. However, some blood clots form inside blood vessels. Most of the time, these blood clots disappear on their own. But sometimes they can be very dangerous.

If a blood clot keeps blood from flowing through blood vessels as it should, organs cannot get the oxygen they need. Without oxygen, organs can't work right. A blood clot in the brain, for example, could damage the part of the brain that can't get oxygen. This is called a stroke. A blood clot that

Most Beautiful Scab

Here is a blood clot in a coronary (heart) artery.

forms in a heart blood vessel can cause a heart attack. If either the brain or the heart is deprived of oxygen long enough, brain damage or death can result.

GANGRENE

All organs and body tissues need blood to bring them oxygen and nutrients. If an organ or tissue loses blood flow for too long, it can die. If that happens to the brain or heart, the person dies. But if it happens in the hands, feet, or other unnecessary body part, the person will live. Just the part dies and begins to decay. **YUM!** This is called gangrene.

For example, let's say you're showing off for friends by spinning a big, huge cinder block on the tip of your finger. Boy, those things are heavy. And then—**WHOOPS!** You drop it on your toe.

When gangrene occurs, skin tissue turns black and dies.

Believe me—**PLEASE DON'T TRY THIS YOURSELF!** A cinder block dropped on a toe is enough to slow or stop blood flow. And if the flow stops for long, yep, **IT'S GANGRENE TIME!**

Gangrene comes in two forms—dry and wet. Both are equally nasty. With dry gangrene, the skin and tissue of your toe slowly dies. It becomes cold and black. It dries out. And after several weeks or a month or so, **THE SKIN AND TISSUE FALL OFF!**

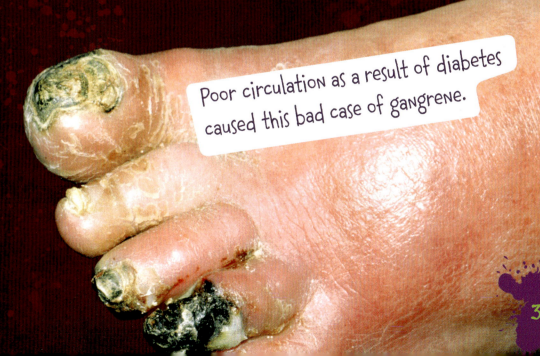

Poor circulation as a result of diabetes caused this bad case of gangrene.

If bacteria, such as this Clostridium bacterium, infect a gangrenous area, you'll end up with pus-covered, wet gangrene. Yikes!

If bacteria invade the toe, you're in even more trouble. The tissue may get infected. When this happens, you have wet gangrene. **LUCKY YOU!** Hardly any blood flows to the toe. So your white blood cells cannot kill the bacteria. Before you know it, the bacteria grow out of control. Your toe begins to rot. Soon it turns black and oozes smelly pus. **YUCK!** Sometimes, doctors have no choice. They have to amputate a toe with gangrene. Yep, the toe has to go.

If it stays, the gangrene could spread to other body parts. Of course, if you get your toe amputated, then you have another problem. What will you do with your old, chopped-off toe? Hang it on your wall? Put it under your pillow for the toe fairy? Or better yet, stick it under your sister's pillow!

MAGGOT THERAPY

Instead of removing a body part that is dead or dying, doctors may put maggots on it. Maggots are fly larvae. These squiggly little white worms are usually found on dead and decaying meat. But they can help the living in three ways. They eat dead tissue, including infected tissue. They give off chemicals that kill bacteria. And they encourage healing.

Not just any maggots will do, however. Only maggots that do not eat healthy tissue or burrow under a person's skin can be used. Otherwise, the person ends up with more problems than before. So next time you put maggots on your decaying flesh, check the label carefully!

IT'S ALL TINGLY

Have you ever gotten out of your chair and almost fallen flat on your face? Your leg has "fallen asleep!" At first, it just feels numb and heavy. You have trouble moving it. But pretty soon it "wakes up" and—*YOW!*—it feels as if somebody's pushing sharp pins into it. That's when you wish it would fall back to sleep.

People usually get this feeling after they put pressure on a part of the body. Maybe you sleep on your arm, or you like to sit with one foot tucked under you. Pressure like that slows down the blood supply. This sends signals to the brain that

Resting your head on your arm can make it fall asleep. And falling asleep in class can get you in real trouble!

something is not quite right with that body part. The tingling feeling is your body's way of saying, "Dude, something's wrong. Time for a change." Without that signal, you might not change positions. And cutting off the blood circulation to any body part for a long time could cause permanent damage.

GROSS FACT #10
The only part of your body that does not have its own blood supply is the cornea of your eye. The cornea gets the oxygen it needs directly from the air.

So don't worry too much if you make hamburger meat out of your arm, leg, or head while riding your bike or skateboard. Most of the time, your blood will take care of everything for you. Oh, except for the pain. You're on your own with that!

Glossary

arteries: blood vessels that carry blood away from the heart

bacteria: very small organisms that can cause infection

blood transfusion: transfer of blood from one person to another person

blood vessels: tubes that carry blood throughout the body

bone marrow: soft, spongy material in the middle of bones where blood cells are made

capillaries: tiny blood vessels that connect arteries and veins

circulatory system: the body system that includes the heart, blood vessels, and all the blood that circulates through the body

hemoglobin: a chemical in red blood cells that carries oxygen

immune system: the body's defense system against infection and disease

infection: the entry and growth of bacteria or other germs inside the body that makes a person sick

platelets: small blood cells necessary for blood clotting

pus: thick liquid containing dead white blood cells that oozes from an infected wound

veins: blood vessels that carry blood back to the heart from other parts of the body

Selected Bibliography

American Academy of Family Physicians. "Nosebleeds." *Familydoctor.org*. December 2006. http://familydoctor.org/online/famdocen/home/healthy/firstaid/basics/132.html#ArticleParsysMiddleColumn0005 (February 28, 2008).

BBC. "Gangrene." *BBC Health*. December 2006. http://www.bbc.co.uk/health/conditions/gangrene1.shtml (February 28, 2008).

Cleveland Clinic Foundation. "Scars: An Overview." *Cleveland Clinic*. March 7, 2005. http://www.clevelandclinic.org/health/health-info/docs/3700/3764.asp?index=11669 (February 28, 2008).

Franklin Institute. "Blood." *Franklin Institute*. N.d. http://www.fi.edu/learn/heart/blood/blood.html (February 28, 2008).

Hayes, Bill. *Five Quarts: A Personal and Natural History of Blood*. New York: Random House Publishing Group, 2005.

Phillips, Roger. "The Heart and the Circulatory System." *National Health Museum*. N.d. http://www.accessexcellence.org/AE/AEC/CC/heart_background.php (February 28, 2008).

Swicofil AG Textile Services. "Sutures." *Swicofil*. N.d. http://www.swicofil.com/sutures.html (February 28, 2008).

U.S. Department of Health and Human Services. "What is Hemophilia?" *National Heart, Lung, and Blood Institute*. June 2007. http://www.nhlbi.nih.gov/health/dci/Diseases/hemophilia/hemophilia_what.html (February 28, 2008).

Further Reading

Ganeri, Anita. *Your Blood*. How Your Body Works series. Mahwah, NJ: World Almanac Books, 2003.
See how your blood flows through your heart and the rest of your circulatory system, mending your wounds and keeping you alive as it goes.

Gordon, Melanie. *Let's Talk about Scratches, Scrapes and Bug Bites*. New York: Rosen Publishing Group, 2003.

Have you been on the bug menu lately? Or have you gotten all scraped and scratched trying to run from the bugs that are trying to munch on you? If so, you need this book. It will tell you how to keep all your wounds from becoming infected.

Johnson, Rebecca L. *Daring Cell Defenders*. Minneapolis: Millbrook Press, 2008.
Discover how your body—including several types of white blood cells—protects you from bacteria and viruses that can make you sick.

Kids Biology
http://www.kidsbiology.com/human_biology/index.php
Read articles and play games about the human body and biology.

Kids Health
http://www.kidshealth.org/kid/
Articles at this website about scars, cuts, scratches, infections, and the immune system are reviewed by physicians and other health experts.

Science News for Kids
http://www.sciencenewsforkids.org/
Find out all the latest news about the human body and other science topics.

Showers, Paul. *Drop of Blood*. New York: HarperCollins Publishers, 2004.
What is in a drop of blood anyway? How does this vital fluid keep you alive? Read this book and find out.

Storad, Conrad. *The Circulatory System*. Minneapolis: Lerner Publications Company, 2005.
Find out how your heart and lungs work together to keep you alive. This book explains the circulatory system, which pumps blood to all of the different parts of the body.

Townsend, John. *Surgery: Scalpels, Stitches and Scars*. Austin, TX: Raintree Publishers, 2005.
Get the gory, grisly facts about the history of medicine. What was it like to have operations before painkillers? Why did barbers make people bleed on purpose? The answers are in this book, and they aren't pretty.

Yount, Lisa. *William Harvey: Discoverer of How Blood Circulates*. Berkeley Heights, NJ: Enslow Publishers, 2008.
Meet the man who dissected enough dead bodies to determine that the heart is a pump capable of squirting blood throughout the body.

INDEX

arteries, 14–16

bacteria, 21, 38. *See also* infection
blood, 6–7, 13–20; circulation of, 18, 35–37, 40–41; donation, 24, 26; loss of, 23–24; transfusion, 24–26; types, 25–26. *See also* blood clot; platelets; red blood cells; white blood cells
blood clot, 5, 34–36
bloodletting, 29–30. *See also* leeches
bloodsuckers, 30–31
blood vessels, 4, 15–16, 27–28, 30, 34–36. *See also* arteries; capillaries; veins
bloodworms, 20
bone marrow, 5
bruises, 32–33; coloring, 33

capillaries, 15–17, 32, 33
clotting, 23; lack of, 28, 30, 31
clotting proteins, 6, 29

gangrene, 36–39; amputation as result of, 38–39

Harvey, William, 18
heart, 14–15, 18
hemoglobin, 19
hemophilia, 28–29

horned lizards, 28

immune system, 21–22
infection, 20–22, 38; fighting, 21

leeches, 30–31
lungs, 14, 17

maggot therapy, 39

nosebleeds, 27–28; causes of, 27–28

platelets, 4–7, 19
pus, 22

red blood cells, 4, 7, 17, 19–20, 33

scab, 7–8, 21, 35
scars, 8–10, 12; keloid, 9; surgical, 9–11
stitches, 10–12; catgut, 11. *See also* surgical staples
surgical staples, 12
sutures. *See* stitches

veins, 14–17

white blood cells, 4, 19–22, 38

About the Author

Kristi Lew is the author of more than two dozen science books for teachers and young people. She studied biochemistry and genetics in college and later worked in genetics laboratories and taught high-school science. When she's not writing, she enjoys sailing with her husband. She writes, lives, and sails in St. Petersburg, Florida.

About the Illustrator

Michael Slack's illustrations have appeared in books, magazines, ads, and on TV. His paintings and drawings have been exhibited in the United States and Europe. Michael lives in the San Francisco Bay area.

Photo Acknowledgments

The images in this book are used with the permission of:© National Cancer Institute/ Photo Researchers, Inc., pp.1 and 3 (background),5 (bottom) ; © Chris Butler/age fotostock/Photolibrary, p. 4; © Volker Steger/Peter Arnold, Inc., p. 7 (top); © Anyka/Shutterstock Images, p. 7 (bottom); © Deb Yeske/Visuals Unlimited, Inc., p. 8; © Mediscan/Visuals Unlimited, Inc., p. 9 (top); Reflexstock/Royalty-free, pp. 9 (bottom), 33 (bottom left inset); © Gustoimages/Photo Researchers, Inc., p. 10; © Eye of Science/Photo Researchers, Inc., p. 11 (top); © Duncan Smith/Photodisc/Getty Images, p. 11 (bottom left); © Dr. P. Marazzi/Photo Researchers, Inc., pp. 11 (center), 38 (bottom);© Cookelma/Dreamstime.com, p. 12 (bottom); © iStockphoto.com/Lisa Sweet, p. 12 (top); © Jim West/The Image Works, p. 13; © Steve Allen/Peter Arnold, Inc., p. 14; © Travisman/Dreamstime.com, p. 15 (top); © A& F Michler/Peter Arnold, Inc., p. 15 (bottom); © Dr. Dennis Kunkel/Visuals Unlimited, Inc., pp. 17,19, 29 (left), 33 (top); © Popperfoto/Getty Images, p. 18 (top); © iStockphoto.com/© Kenneth C. Zirkel, p. 18 (bottom); © Knorre/Shutterstock Images, p. 20 (top); © Edgewater Media/Shutterstock Images, p. 20 (bottom); © CDC/Custom Medical Stock Photo , p. 21; © Simko/Visuals Unlimited, Inc., p. 22 (top); © Custom Medical Stock Photo , p. 22 (bottom); © Davies and Starr/Getty Images, p. 24; © Dr. Barry Slaven/Visuals Unlimited, Inc., p. 25; © Medicimage/The Medical File/Peter Arnold, Inc., p. 26; © John Cancalosi/naturepl.com, p. 28 (top); © jathys/Shutterstock Images, p. 28 (bottom); © Devonyu/Dreamstime.com, p. 29 (right); © Scientifica/Visuals Unlimited, Inc., p. 30; © Bruce Dale/ National Geographic/Getty Images, p. 31 (top); © iStockphoto.com/Lev Ezhov, p. 31 (center left); © Medical RF/The Medical File/Peter Arnold, Inc., p. 31 (bottom); © iStockphoto.com/© Berit Skogmo, p. 32; © iStockphoto.com/Dave Long, p. 33 (bottom right inset); © iStockphoto.com/Dimitri Mordolff, p. 33 (center right inset); © worldthroughthelens-medical/Alamy, p. 33 (top right inset); © Robert Caughey/Visuals Unlimited, Inc., p. 34; © CNRI/Photo Researchers, Inc., p. 35 (bottom); © Mike Delvin/Photo Researchers, Inc., p. 37; © Dr Gopal Murti/Photo Researchers, Inc., p. 38 (top); © Imagesource/Getty Images, p. 40; © Just_Human/Dreamstime.com, p. 41 (top); © PhotoAlto/Laurence Mouton/Getty Images, p. 41 (bottom).

Front cover: © iStockphoto.com/Sharon Dominick (teenager with pained expression); © iStockphoto.com/cloki (band-aid on forehead); © Stockxpert (injured arm), © The Guitar Man/Dreamstime.com (maggots); © Adrian Hillman/Dreamstime.com (veins); © iStockphoto.com/Mikhail Malyshev (leeches); © iStockphoto.com/Bogdan Pop (red blood cells); KYU OH/stock exclusive/Getty Images (background micrograph).